A Donation has been made to the
Clay County Public Library by:

The Celina High Class of 1955

TECH PIONEERS™

MARC ANDREESSEN

CORONA BREZINA

ROSEN
PUBLISHING

NEW YORK

Published in 2016 by The Rosen Publishing Group, Inc.
29 East 21st Street, New York, NY 10010

Copyright © 2016 by The Rosen Publishing Group, Inc.

First Edition

Library of Congress Cataloging-in-Publication Data

Brezina, Corona, author.
Marc Andreessen / Corona Brezina. — First Edition.
    pages cm. — (Tech pioneers)
Includes bibliographical references and index.
ISBN 978-1-4994-6284-5 (library bound)
1. Andreessen, Marc—Juvenile literature. 2. Computer programmers—United States—Biography—Juvenile literature. 3. Web services—Juvenile literature. I. Title.
TK5102.56.A53B74 2015
338.7'6100571376092—dc23
[B]
                          2015033179

Manufactured in the United States of America

CONTENTS

On May 23, 2014, Marc Andreessen had some opinions to share on
what the future held for civiliza-
tion. Characteristically, he turned to Twitter
to make his points. "1/A tweetstorm in four
parts: The 'superpowers' metaphor for how
new technologies enhance human capabilities," he began. Next, "2/New technologies
can be thought of as giving people superpowers—superhuman abilities that humans
did not have before." By the end of the first
part, he'd concluded that, "10/For 500+ years,
we've collectively been radically enhancing
capabilities of ordinary humans through
technology superpowers."

Andreessen is well qualified to discuss
the transformative potential of technology.
In the early 1990s, when he was just out of
college, he founded the company Netscape,
which produced the first computer web
browser that achieved mainstream popularity.
tion made the World Wide Web widely acce
helped usher in the Internet age.

Marc Andreessen speaks at the 2014 Vanity Fair New Establishment Summit about ideas and innovations shaping the future—a perfect subject for his expertise.

Back then, he was viewed as a young tech prodigy, the founder of one of the first Internet companies that sprang up during the 1990s. Today, Andreessen sometimes refers to the stages of his life as versions of a software product. The "Marc 1.0," who established Netscape as a newcomer to the tech world of Silicon Valley in California, has given way to today's "Marc 3.0," a well-connected insider in the valley. In between, "Marc 2.0" learned entrepreneurship and watched tech trends evolve.

Netscape folded, but Andreessen has since established himself as a venture capitalist aiming to support the next start-ups inventing the innovative tech products of tomorrow. Andreessen has a knack for forecasting some of the technology trends of the near future. After the rapid growth of the Internet in the 1990s, Andreessen anticipated the arrival of cloud computing and social media. He now predicts that computer software will continue to transform sectors of the economy, from national defense to education to health care.

Here is his final wrap-up of his "tech gives people superpowers" tweetstorm: "13/My nomination: Tech-driven price deflation; lowers prices, reduces measured GDP & productivity, while boosting consumer welfare." In Andreessen's view, tech innovations have the potential to create a bright future, and he aims to be one of the people making it possible.

Chapter One

The Dawn of the Age of Computing

Silicon Valley, in Northern California, is the unofficial capital of the U.S. technology sector. It is home to many of the world's leading tech companies, including Apple, Google, Hewlett-Packard, Intel, and Facebook. Silicon Valley is also the epicenter of tech start-up companies trying to set themselves up as the next big breakout. Although the region had a long history of technology development, during the 1990s Silicon Valley became closely associated in the public mind with the explosive growth of the Internet. Some of the founders of the prominent Internet companies are widely familiar today—most people know Apple cofounder Steve Jobs and Facebook founder Mark Zuckerberg.

The name Marc Andreessen is less recognized. Within Silicon Valley, though, he is well-known as a champion for technology's potential to transform entire sectors of the economy. Kevin Roose of *New York* magazine once described him as "Silicon Valley's resident philosopher-king." But the ultimate insider actually established his reputation before Silicon Valley became a hub for tech innovation and before he migrated west to California.

ANDREESSEN'S EARLY LIFE

Marc Lowell Andreessen spent his formative early years in the Midwest. He was born in Cedar Falls, Iowa, on July 9, 1971. He had one sibling, a brother named Jeff. When Marc was two years old, his family moved to New Lisbon, Wisconsin, where they lived ten miles (sixteen kilometers) outside of the small town. Andreessen grew up among hardworking farmers who depended on the long-term success of their crops for their livelihoods. His mother worked in customer service for the catalog clothing retailer Land's End. His father was a sales manager for a seed company. Long before becoming a billionaire, Andreessen held low-paying jobs washing dishes, working retail, mowing lawns, and doing farm labor.

Andreessen had a happy childhood, although he was fascinated by technology while growing up in a small town where many of his peers were focused on football and other athletics. Despite reaching a height of six feet

Andreessen learned the value of hard work growing up in rural Wisconsin. One winter, when his family relied on a woodstove for heat, he helped chop firewood.

four inches (193 centimeters), Andreessen was more interested in reading science fiction books than playing sports in high school.

At New Lisbon High School, Andreessen impressed his teachers with his imagination, intellect, and humor. Even as a high school student, he had confidence in his own unconventional ideas, and he didn't mind criticizing some of the assignments that his teachers handed out. He excelled in school, and he became a National Merit Scholar.

Andreessen's town didn't have a bookstore, and it had only a small public library. There were only a handful of TV channels and radio stations. Looking back, it's not surprising that the boy who was starved for information grew up to help make the Internet accessible to the masses.

Introducing the PC

When he was in fifth grade, Andreessen spent time recuperating from an operation. For most twelve-year-olds, the experience would be a painful childhood memory. But for Andreessen, it was an opportunity. He convinced his parents to buy him a TRS-80, an early mass-produced computer, from Radio Shack during his recovery, and he developed a passion for programming.

Owning his own computer put the Wisconsin farm boy in a small, tech-savvy minority. Personal computers (PCs) had only recently become affordable for the general public. Compared to today's computers and smartphones, they were primitive and unwieldy. Data was stored on small hard drives—typically 10 megabytes or fewer—or on even smaller floppy disk drives. They had text-based user interfaces, meaning that users had to type in commands sequentially, rather than the graphical user interfaces used in most computers and handheld devices today. Most did not have color displays, they generally did not connect to networks, and many required that users do at least some of their own programming. But the generation that grew up with these computers became the key innovators in the new world of the Internet.

Early computers used the programming language BASIC. Andreessen taught himself programming from a

Now a museum piece, the TRS-80 computer sold by Radio Shack was one of the best-selling PCs during the late 1970s and early 1980s.

library book and spent his money from summer jobs on computer magazines. Once, when he was writing a program on a school computer to do his math homework, he lost his work because the janitor turned off the building's electricity. By middle school, he was creating games for his family's new cutting-edge Commodore 64 computer.

Andreessen made it clear to his friends that he planned to leave rural life behind him after he graduated from high school. He chose to attend the University of Illinois at Urbana-Champaign, which he later described to Claire Cain Miller of *SFGate* as having "cornfields on three sides and a pig farm on the fourth side." Regardless,

Serious early computer users could create their own programs using BASIC. The mouse didn't yet exist, but a joystick could be added onto many early models.

the school also has one of the top computer science programs in the United States.

DIALING UP THE INTERNET

Despite his interest in computers, Andreessen did not
intend to major in computer science when he began college. He planned to pursue electrical engineering. Jobs
in the field paid well, and the University of Illinois had a
highly regarded electrical engineering program. Andreessen later claimed that the only reason he switched to
computer science was that it required less work. He also
enjoyed taking intellectually stimulating classes unrelated to his major, such as philosophy and English. Later
in life, Andreessen would become known for the wide
breadth of his interests and opinions.

During his senior year, Andreessen left his
slacker habits behind when he became involved in a
project that required long, intensive hours behind
the computer. It began when he got a programming
job that paid $6.85 an hour at the National Center for
Supercomputing Applications (NCSA). His official
assignment was to work on developing a visualization program that would run on supercomputers. But
Andreessen wasn't interested in advances in supercomputing. During an internship at IBM, he had worked
on the development of a new workstation computer.

NATIONAL CENTER FOR SUPERCOMPUTING APPLICATIONS (NCSA)

The National Center for Supercomputing Applications (NCSA), affiliated with the University of Illinois, provides scientists and engineers with the opportunity to use supercomputers in their research. The history of the NCSA began in the 1980s, when astrophysicist Larry Smarr wrote to the National Science Foundation (NSF) about the lack of supercomputing power in the United States. In response to Smarr's comment, the NSF formed a new Office for Advanced Scientific Computing. In 1985, the office announced the creation of five supercomputing centers across the country.

The NCSA opened in 1986, led by Smarr. Almost immediately, the center became well-known for Telnet, an early communication program. It also established itself as a leader in visualization—the use of software to translate data into images. Today, the NCSA continues to serve as a cutting-edge research institution. The facility's Cray supercomputer Blue Waters, wich was installed in 2012, is one of the fastest supercomputers in the world.

The experience had convinced him that the future lay with smaller machines.

Andreessen also began to explore the Internet when he arrived at the NCSA. He hadn't had access to the Internet in his Wisconsin hometown, and even if a connection had been available, it would have been slow dial-up access. The NCSA, however, provided broadband Internet connectivity that wouldn't be widely accessible for the general public until the early twenty-first century.

At that time, the Internet was mostly the realm of academics and computer experts. It connected computer users across the world, but it took expertise to access information. Transferring files, for example, generally required knowledge of commands used by the Unix operating system. The Internet had great commercial potential, Andreessen thought, but it was too complicated for most people to use for everyday transactions.

After he began working at the NCSA, Andreessen became aware of a new information system being developed called the World Wide Web. Today, most people would be hard-pressed to describe the difference between the Internet and the World Wide Web. But the two terms are not interchangeable. The Internet is the global infrastructure of computer networks. The World Wide Web is a means of disseminating information over the Internet.

Computer scientist Tim Berners-Lee created the web, as it's commonly called, in 1989. Frustrated by the complicated sequences necessary to access files, he aimed to simplify the process. His web consisted of web pages designated by address codes called universal resource locators (URLs). Pages were created by hypertext markup language (HTML) and transferred using hypertext transfer protocol (HTTP). One of Berners-Lee's most crucial decisions was ideological, not technical. He advocated for a free, open web that did not charge fees or restrict use.

Berners-Lee's web provided the architecture for exchanging information, but it was not yet user-friendly. He released a basic web browser that displayed little more than lines of text. To Berners-Lee, the World Wide Web

Tim Berners-Lee, inventor of the World Wide Web, defends the open Internet and discusses the rise of the social Web at a 2012 conference.

TIM BERNERS-LEE

Tim Berners-Lee (1955–) is a British computer scientist known for inventing the World Wide Web in 1989. A graduate of Oxford University, Berners-Lee spent a six-month fellowship at CERN, the European Particle Physics Laboratory, in 1980. During that time, as a side project, he wrote a program called Enquire that organized information as an assortment of linked documents. Berners-Lee returned to CERN later in the 1980s, where he was often frustrated by the complicated process of accessing data on the Internet. He proposed applying the principles behind Enquire, which dealt with CERN's system, to the entire Internet. He called his global hypertext project the World Wide Web, and in 1991, the world's first website, http://info.cern.ch, explained the concepts behind the World Wide Web project.

In 1994, Berners-Lee founded the World Wide Web Consortium, the organization that develops the technical standards for the World Wide Web. Today, he continues to serve as its director.

was a research tool. Other people grasped its commercial potential. For the general public to gain access to the web, however, the interface would have to be made easier and more enjoyable to use.

Andreessen saw traces of elitism in the academic vision of the World Wide Web. It seemed that some computer experts opposed making the web more accessible to the masses. The web felt like an exclusive club that required computer expertise. Andreessen spoke of how "There was a definite element of not wanting to make it easier, of actually wanting to keep the riffraff out," as John Cassidy explained in his book *Dot.con.*

A similar split had occurred upon the development of graphic user interfaces for desktop computers. Instead of typing out complicated lines of text, users could simply click on icons and other graphical elements with a computer mouse. Apple released the first graphic user interfaces in the 1980s, marketing its computer as a user-friendly product. Rates of computer ownership increased sharply in the 1990s.

Several computer scientists released their own browsers for the World Wide Web, but they were difficult to obtain or had other flaws that kept them from becoming widely popular. Andreessen corresponded with the creator of one of these early browsers, offering ideas for improvements, but the scientist would not collaborate on modifying his program. Andreessen then became determined to create his own web browser that would make the web accessible and easy to use for everyone.

Chapter Two

NAVIGATING THE NET

I n the fall semester of 1992, Andreessen was formally assigned the project of developing a new web browser that combined graphics as well as text. Andreessen had managed to recruit a collaborator who was equally avid about the project. Eric Bina was a brilliant NCSA programmer who couldn't resist the challenge.

Andreessen and Bina began spending long hours at their computers as they tackled the project. There were no windows in their workspace, so they barely knew whether it was day or night outside. Andreessen survived on milk and Pepperidge Farm cookies; Bina preferred Skittles candy and Mountain Dew. Later on, as more programmers joined the effort, pizza boxes started to pile up in stacks around the room. If Andreessen was gone from their basement workspace for more than a few hours, someone would go to his apartment to rouse him. As the frantic eighteen-hour days passed by, the lines of code for the new browser added up and began to resemble a functional program.

Inventing Mosaic

Andreessen wanted the new browser to display web pages in a format comparable to the pages of a magazine. It would provide the option of different fonts and font sizes. Instead of displaying text as though it were being entered by a typewriter, the browser would mix text and graphics on a point-and-click interface. The difficulty was that the software for creating graphical web browsers wouldn't allow the features Andreessen wanted. Bina, who wrote most of the code for the project, solved the problem by customizing a new tool now called HTML Layout Widget.

Bina and Andreessen disagreed about whether or not the new browser should allow the option of including images. Andreessen argued that featuring photographs on websites would prove highly popular. Bina thought that posting images on the Internet would mostly be a waste of space. Bina was overruled, and their web browser allowed pictures to be displayed. (Andreessen later claimed that a few months after Mosaic was released, Tim Berners-Lee chastised him for including images, because people were taking advantage of the feature for trivial purposes like putting family photographs online.)

Meanwhile, Andreessen worked to ensure that the browser would be able to connect to all of the different types of computer servers across the world. He also designed the appearance and controls. Above all, he aimed to make it user-friendly. The user would be able to access a hypertext link simply by clicking the mouse. It had Forward and Back buttons and allowed users to cancel a connection if it stalled or they changed their minds.

Andreessen and Bina completed a preliminary version of their new browser in about two months. According to John Cassidy's book *Dot.con*, on January 23, 1993, Andreessen sent out a message to an online discussion group: "By the power vested in me by nobody in particular, alpha/beta version 0.5 of NCSA's Motif-based networked information systems and World Wide Web browser, X Mosaic, is hereby released. Cheers, Marc."

Mosaic—the X was later dropped—is sometimes incorrectly credited with being the first graphical web browser. There had been earlier graphical browsers, but they did not succeed because obtaining or using them was difficult. Mosaic finally made the web easily accessible, as was demonstrated by its nearly instant popularity.

REACHING THE PUBLIC

Within ten minutes of Andreessen's message, the first user downloaded Mosaic. Within the hour, a hundred people had downloaded it, and Andreessen was already receiving positive feedback. A couple of days later, Berners-Lee praised Mosaic as "brilliant" and added it to the CERN website for users to download. Mosaic continued to pique interest. In February of 1993, more than a thousand people downloaded the browser.

Its popularity was partly because Mosaic was free. Since NCSA was funded by the government, the browser was not intended to be a commercial product. In addition, the code was open source. This meant that anybody could read through the code to figure out how the Mosaic team had constructed the program. Andreessen encouraged users to report bugs and make suggestions for new features. He used the feedback as he worked to improve the browser.

The initial version could be used only on Unix computers. After Mosaic proved a success, NCSA began assigning more resources to the project. Programmers were assigned to write versions of Mosaic for Macintosh and Windows. By November of 1993, all three versions had been released to the public, making Mosaic accessible to anybody who owned their own desktop computer. Thousands of people rushed to download the new versions, and the number reached about a million by the end of the year.

The rapid growth achieved another of Andreessen's goals in producing a user-friendly browser. He wanted to encourage ordinary people to create content for the web. Early on, some computer scientists argued that there was no point in increasing access to the Internet because there wasn't much online that would interest the general public. Academic institutions had created most of the documents. But as more people downloaded Mosaic, they began publishing their own websites. In early 1993, fewer than one hundred commercial websites existed. By the end of the year, there were more than ten thousand.

As Mosaic grew into a phenomenon, management figures at NCSA started monitoring the project more closely. Andreessen and the other programmers began to feel marginalized. A *New York Times* article quoted Smarr extensively, but Andreessen and the original Mosaic creators did not get mentioned.

MOVING WEST

In December of 1993, Andreessen graduated from college. He asked NCSA if he could continue working at the center, and they made him a generous job offer. But they also included the condition that Andreessen would not be involved in Mosaic. He declined the offer.

Andreessen had established a reputation for himself in the tech world, and he did not have to worry about a shortage of job offers. He also knew that he wanted to work in the private sector, not academia. He accepted

JIM CLARK

Andreessen founded Netscape in partnership with tech entrepreneur Jim Clark (1944–). Clark wanted to work with Andreessen because he saw him as a visionary who had innovative ideas about future high-tech ventures. Clark brought considerable technical expertise and long experience working in Silicon Valley. A physicist and computer scientist, Clark taught at the University of California and Stanford University during the 1970s and early 1980s. In 1982, he left academia to found Silicon Graphics, Inc. (SGI), which created special effects for movies such as *Jurassic Park*. The company proved a massive success, but Clark left in 1994. He wanted to explore the mass-market potential of the Internet. The result was Netscape.

After his involvement in Netscape ended, Clark founded a health care software company that later merged with WebMD and a wealth management company, myCFO, that was later acquired by BMO Harris Bank. Clark also made investments in Apple that returned him to the Forbes Billionaires List in 2012.

a position at an e-commerce security company in Silicon Valley called Enterprise Integration Technologies.

In January, he moved out to California and started his new programming job. Andreessen considered himself finished with Mosaic.

Andreessen did not stay with Enterprise Integration Technologies for long. Shortly after arriving in California, he received an e-mail from Jim Clark, founder of Silicon Graphics, Inc. (SGI), stating that he was planning to start a new company and wanted to meet Andreessen. Clark had only just heard of Marc Andreessen, and he used

Jim Clark, shown in 1996, taught computer science at Stanford and held the position of chief technical officer at SGI before cofounding Netscape.

Mosaic for the first time to locate Andreessen's e-mail address on his home page.

Clark asked Andreessen to join him in starting up a new software company. They decided that they would focus on the commercial prospects of the Internet. In those early days, many people doubted that the Internet could ever support any profitable ventures. Clark and Andreessen believed that the Internet held great promise, but before it could be realized, potential customers needed a better way to access online content. Specifically, Clark believed, they required a commercial successor to Mosaic that was faster, more powerful, and more satisfying to use.

INTRODUCING NETSCAPE NAVIGATOR

Clark and Andreessen started out by calling their new company Mosaic Communications. NCSA later raised legal objections to their use of "Mosaic," so it was eventually changed to Netscape.

The name wasn't the only thing they appropriated from NCSA—they also quickly hired many of the original Mosaic programmers. Clark offered them a generous salary as well as stock options. The offer of stock options meant that if the company went public, they would all be given the opportunity to buy shares of stock. If the company was a success, the value of the stock could rise significantly and make them rich. Clark also hired some of his colleagues from SGI.

When Bina and the other original programmers resigned from NCSA, they were unaware that NCSA was negotiating to license the Mosaic code to a start-up called Spyglass. Competition between rival browser companies was already beginning to simmer.

Within a week, Clark rented space for the new company's headquarters in an office building in Mountain View. Clark and Andreessen had only a vague business plan. Their first priority was to release a new browser as quickly as possible. Millions of people were flocking to the web, and Clark and Andreessen did not want Mosaic to become the default favorite browser for novice Internet users.

They would have to write the code for the new browser from scratch because NCSA owned the Mosaic code. The programmers already had plans for improvements that would make the final product faster and more

Programmers who created Netscape Navigator included cybersecurity measures even though most people hadn't yet heard of hackers or thought about online privacy.

reliable. They also planned to incorporate security measures into the software, which was a brand-new idea for the time. Any information being transmitted online would be encrypted to prevent it from being intercepted by hackers.

Another key difference between Mosaic and Netscape was that Andreessen and Clark started out with the goal of making a profit. They would give the browser away for free, but they would sell related software to businesses. They also considered the possibility of selling advertisements.

As the media speculated about the nature of Clark's new venture—reporters frequently called to ask questions—the programming team started work. Andreessen and Clark hired managers and more programmers. The team settled down to work 120-hour weeks. Several futon mattresses were installed in the office for when programmers needed to crash. Sometimes they would take a break to play air hockey, race remote-controlled cars, or even to leave the building for a meal or a shower. But most of their time was spent at the computers creating code. In addition to programming and planning new features for Netscape, Andreessen also spent time dealing with the media.

Meanwhile, Clark needed to secure financial backing that would pay the bills during the early development period. Clark had wanted to avoid involving venture capitalists in the new company. Venture capitalists are investors who provide capital to start-up companies to make money if they eventually succeed. Clark was concerned that venture capitalists could demand too much control of the company while drawing off its financial returns. Still, he turned to John Doerr of the venture capital firm Kleiner Perkins Caufield and Byers. Doerr agreed to make an investment of $5 million in exchange for shares of stock. Clark and Doerr also hired a CEO for

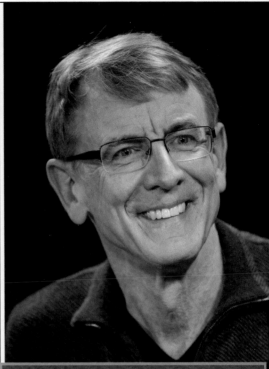

Legendary venture capitalist John Doerr directed his firm's investments in many successful start-ups, including Compaq, Sun Microsystems, Google, Amazon, and Uber.

the company. Jim Barksdale was a respected telecommunications executive.

NETSCAPE SETS SAIL

By August of 1994, the programmers had the new browser up and running. To make sure it was running properly, Netscape hired testers to try it out and identify problems. They would surf the web and test all of the browser's features. Finally, the programmers compared the new browser's performance against Mosaic. They were thrilled to see that their browser was faster and more visually appealing.

October 13, 1994, was a momentous day: Mosaic Netscape 0.9 officially set sail. The team who had created the browser all gathered together in the conference room and burst into excited cheers at the exact moment of release.

Chapter Three

THE BROWSER WARS

I n 1996, *Time* magazine featured Marc Andreessen on the cover of the February 19 issue of the magazine— an incredible piece of recognition for a man who was only twenty-four years old. He was shown sitting on an ornate red velvet and gold throne. He's wearing jeans and a T-shirt, and his feet are bare. The headline read, "The Golden Geeks: They invent. They start companies. And the stock market has made them INSTANTAIRES. Who are they? How do they live? And what do they mean for America's future?"

To the public, Andreessen was far more than just a brilliant young tech visionary. He was the public face of Netscape, and Netscape represented the sudden intro- duction of the web into people's daily lives. Some consid- ered it an invasion.

At the onset of the dot-com boom in the mid-1990s, Marc Andreessen became a public face for the new era of the Internet.

Andreessen was personally thriving as well. Despite the *Time* magazine photo, he'd mainly given up the clothes from his student days for expensive suits. He now drove a Mercedes-Benz and owned a Mediterranean-style house where he lived with his girlfriend and three bulldogs. Once, his girlfriend dyed one of the dogs teal to match the Netscape logo. Andreessen had established a reputation for being an intensely private person, and the couple tended to spend their leisure time at home rather than going out.

But even at the height of Netscape's prosperity, the company was still scrambling to churn out products that would turn a profit and keep the loyalty of users. Microsoft Corporation had been monitoring Netscape's extraordinary success, and the two companies were locked in fierce competition.

AN INSTANT SENSATION

Mosaic Netscape 0.9 quickly received positive reviews from users. But that version of the browser was only the beta release, which meant that it was still being tested, adjusted, and finalized. Andreessen had set the goal of releasing the commercial version by the end of the year. It was crucial for Netscape's success that they finish work on a product that could make a profit. The telephone company called MCI had already expressed an interest in

NAVIGATOR'S LEGACY: FROM COOKIES TO FIREFOX

In addition to its cultural contribution toward democratizing the Internet, Netscape developed important technical innovations for its Navigator browser. A Netscape programmer invented HTML cookies (usually just called cookies), which are small pieces of tracking software that a server installs on a user's computer when a he or she visits its website. Later, another programmer developed JavaScript, the programming language used to develop websites. (JavaScript is not related to the Java computer programming language.)

A descendent of Navigator lives on, as well, in the Mozilla Firefox browser. In 1998, Netscape had made the source code for Communicator public in the hope that outside software developers could suggest new innovations. The move failed to save the company, but it created a project called Mozilla to promote open source software development. (The name had a long history for Netscape. In the 1990s, during the development of the original browser, the programmers had nicknamed it Mozilla, for "Mosaic Killer." Its mascot was a monster that resembled Godzilla.) Despite Mozilla's connection to Netscape, however, the Firefox browser was not based on the Netscape code.

providing Netscape to users signing up for its new Internet service.

Netscape Navigator 1.0 was made available on December 15. It quickly became one of the most popular pieces of software ever created. Four months after its release, six million copies had been downloaded. Seventy-five percent of Internet users were running Navigator. By mid-1995, ten million people were using Netscape Navigator, a number that would grow to thirty-eight million a year later. At its height, Netscape would claim 88 percent of the browser market.

According to the license agreement, users were expected to pay for Navigator after using it for three months. There was no means of enforcement, but many people paid anyway. The company also began to make money by selling software related to Navigator, such as servers for websites. Eventually, 70 percent of big Fortune 100 companies bought Netscape products.

In August of 1995, Netscape officially went public and made its initial public offering (IPO). Going public means that a company sells shares of its stock for the first time, often raising a huge amount of capital as a result. Buying stock during an IPO is sometimes considered a risky move for investors because young companies may fail to thrive. An IPO represents a turning point for a company as well because its leaders are now accountable to stockholders.

It was almost unheard of for a company like Netscape to go public after just fifteen months, especially because it had not proven that its business model could make a profit. Netscape's IPO was one of the most high-profile debuts of a company in history. It was the first IPO of a so-called dot-com, or an Internet-related tech company.

On the day of the IPO, shares went from an initial price of $28 to a high of $74.75. By the end of the day, the company was valued at $4.4 billion. The IPO had broken records. Clark, who had invested millions of dollars of his own money in Netscape, was now worth over half a billion dollars. Andreessen woke up in the midmorning, which was early for him, and checked the value of his shares online. He discovered that he was worth $70 million, and then he went back to sleep. (The figure settled down to $58.3 million by the end of the day.)

After the IPO, Netscape continued its ascent. It moved into bigger headquarters in Mountain View. The number of employees climbed from the hundreds into the thousands, and the company needed more buildings for office space. The value of a Netscape stock share reached its peak in December, at $171. Navigator 1.0 was succeeded by the successful Navigator 2.0. Netscape began acquiring smaller companies that produced Internet software. The company was making solid profits selling software for the computer servers of big corporations.

A GIANT COMPETITOR

Netscape had achieved a stable financial situation, but its success had drawn the attention of a rival. The software giant Microsoft Corporation was targeting Netscape by developing and promoting its own web browser.

In the 1990s, Microsoft was the undisputed leader in the computer software market. The wealthiest company in the world, it did not have any major competitors, in part because Microsoft crushed potential competitors. Still, Bill Gates, the chairman of Microsoft, was slow to recognize the potential of the Internet and the World Wide Web. He thought that the web would just be a short-lived form of using the Internet. He did not anticipate that it would become the dominant means of using online resources, largely due to the popularity of Netscape.

Before Netscape's IPO, Netscape representatives had met with a team from Microsoft to discuss the possibility of a partnership. Microsoft offered to buy a significant stake in Netscape in return for a seat on its board of directors. Netscape would also have to keep Microsoft informed of the company's plans. They discussed the possibility of making Netscape compatible with the upcoming release of the Windows computer operating system, but the Microsoft representatives wouldn't divulge any details about the operating system unless Netscape agreed to their terms. Andreessen, who attended the meeting, thought that the proposal sounded coercive, or threatening. The partnership negotiations came to nothing.

Netscape's success demonstrated two things to Microsoft. It was possible to make money on the Internet. And the new dot-com model based on online enterprises could eventually prove to be a threat to Microsoft's empire founded on software.

In 1995, Microsoft released the newest version of its Windows operating system, which was a huge commercial success. At the same time, it released its own web browser. Internet Explorer was based on Spyglass Mosaic, created by Spyglass, Inc., which had licensed the original Mosaic code from NCSA.

With the introduction of Internet Explorer, Gates intended to make his browser as dominant for using the Internet as Windows was for desktop computing. Although Microsoft lagged behind Netscape on the quality of its browser, the $300 billion company's vast resources gave it an advantage.

THE BATTLE FOR MARKET SHARE

Unlike Netscape, Microsoft did not need to earn a profit on its Internet software. The company made plenty of money on its other software products. Therefore, once

Gates put his mind to conquering the Internet, he was able to devote Microsoft's resources toward the goal without worrying about the cost. He set twenty thousand people to work on Internet projects. Microsoft could afford to give away the browser and other web products for free

In a 1997 publicity photo, Marc Andreessen stands behind the captain's wheel of a ship, a symbol used in the icon for the Netscape Navigator browser.

in order to gain more users than Netscape. The company was also powerful enough that it could convince telecom companies to favor Internet Explorer over Navigator.

Microsoft's efforts began to succeed. Internet Explorer 3.0, which incorporated many of the same features as Navigator, was equivalent in quality to Netscape Navigator 3.0. Both browsers were released in August of 1996. Microsoft began requiring that computers sold with the Windows operating system also come with Internet Explorer installed. Gates thought if users already had a browser ready to use on their desktop, they wouldn't go through the trouble of seeking out an alternative. Statistics proved him correct. From 1995 to early 1998, Navigator's share of users fell from 80 percent to 60 percent. Internet Explorer's share rose from 5 percent to 40 percent. In August, Internet Explorer surpassed Navigator in popularity.

Netscape retaliated by introducing more features and products. In 1996, it released Netscape Communicator. Early on, Andreessen had proposed bundling the browser with other Internet products, such as newsgroups and e-mail capabilities. Communicator achieved this goal, but Netscape's products were no longer cutting-edge and innovative. Microsoft was gradually integrating Explorer and Internet capabilities into its Windows operating system. And as Netscape packed more features into the browser, performance became

Netscape attempted a variety of strategies to combat Microsoft's advances in the browser market, including giving Andreessen a bigger management role.

41

slower and less reliable. The company was in turmoil. Profits and deadlines slipped.

In 1997, the company attempted to remedy a missed opportunity by reintroducing its website as Netcenter. The Netscape home page had always been heavily trafficked, but the site lacked significant content and attractions for users. Now Netscape hoped to make it a destination where users could find information and entertainment.

In 1996, Netscape had formally accused Microsoft of anticompetitive practices. The Department of Justice began an antitrust investigation and filed a lawsuit against Microsoft in 1998. The case was finally settled in 2001, but the decision came too late to affect Netscape.

Meanwhile, Andreessen had lost his own sense of direction within the company. His official job title was chief technology officer. He hadn't written any code since 1994, but he didn't have much of a voice in management decisions either. In 1998, after an $88 million quarterly loss that meant the company was forced to fire hundreds of employees, Andreessen was promoted to executive vice president. At the time, he stated that he welcomed the opportunity to take on management responsibilities. Later on, however, he admitted that he didn't think he had the best temperament for the position of managing company operations.

At a 2001 conference, Marc Andreessen speaks about "Leadership in Turbulent Times," a topic that accurately describes the Netscape era of his life.

43

AHEAD OF HIS TIME?

In November of 1998, the announcement came that Netscape was being sold to America Online (AOL). Although the $4.2 billion deal was essentially an admission that Microsoft had won the browser wars, the terms guaranteed financial security for Netscape employees. They received shares of AOL stock at a time when the company was on an ascent. Under the new owner, Netscape quickly declined into insignificance.

Andreessen took the position of AOL's chief technology officer, where he found himself bewildered by the company's lack of vision. Most AOL customers accessed the Internet using the company's dial-up service. Andreessen thought that the company should aim to offer faster means of connection, such as broadband Internet or DSL connections. AOL management focused instead on content, believing that if customers were satisfied with the AOL experience, they wouldn't be tempted to sign up for faster Internet service. Andreessen left AOL in September of 1999, shortly before the company's merger with Time Warner. The Netscape Navigator browser was formally abandoned in 2008.

Netscape was an iconic product of its time, but it was also, in a sense, ahead of its time. Andreessen held that, eventually, computer operating systems would become irrelevant. Programs would instead run on the browser.

Gates recognized this possibility and the threat it posed to Microsoft's operating systems and computer software. And Andreessen claimed that the Internet would make Windows obsolete. Andreessen was correct about the trend of programs being run by browsers rather than operating systems, although the migration began to take place well into the 2000s. Today, people check e-mail, write documents, and participate in social media on the browsers of their digital devices—but they don't use Netscape to do it.

Chapter Four

MOVING UP TO THE CLOUD

Even before Marc Andreessen left AOL, he was thinking of starting another company. Three of Andreessen's former Netscape employees were interested in joining him in his new venture as well. As the group talked about possible ideas for the new company, one of the men complained about his job at AOL. There were bugs in the e-commerce system, and it tended to crash. Getting the software to a huge number of users was a complicated process.

One of the four wondered, what if there was a company that could provide software and services to Internet businesses so that they wouldn't have to worry about the maintenance of their sites? Part of their services was what came to be known as cloud computing. Back in 1999, the cloud—and Loudcloud, the company founded by Andreessen and his cofounders—was an innovative new concept.

A Cloud on the Horizon

In cloud computing, the "cloud" is the Internet. Instead of storing programs and data on a hard drive—known as local storage—everything is accessed online. The services are provided by a system of servers. As mentioned, social media sites such as Twitter and Facebook are examples of cloud computing, as are webmail services such as Gmail. Streaming media, such as Netflix, use the cloud. You don't

Cloud computing service providers can benefit individuals and businesses by offering products and capabilities that are convenient, flexible, and cost-effective.

need to buy a DVD player and a disc—both the application and the data are provided over the Internet.

Until the twenty-first century, almost all computing used local storage. Cloud computing would not be feasible without the fast Internet connections that have become almost universally available. Today, local computing and cloud computing may overlap, such as with a hard drive that is backed up by cloud storage or applications that automatically access the Internet for some features.

Cloud computing has become a huge business that continues to experience rapid growth. Many major tech companies have introduced cloud services. Google Drive provides online apps and storage, as does Apple's cloud service, iCloud. Google also produces a computer, the Chromebook, in which the operating system is essentially browser based—just as Marc Andreessen predicted.

For consumers, cloud computing is convenient. For businesses, however, it is often transformative. Before the cloud, companies had to buy computers and load them with programs for every employee. When hardware and software became obsolete, they had to be upgraded. Cloud computing allows a more efficient use of shared resources, such as access to servers. If a business expands or contracts, access to the cloud is easily adapted. Sharing data is easier over the cloud. Several service categories are available to businesses, including infrastructure as a service (IaaS), platform as a service (PaaS), and software as a service (SaaS). A cloud can be public, private (used by a single organization), or hybrid (a mix of both).

LOUDCLOUD'S AMBITION

When Andreessen started thinking about starting a company that used cloud computing, however, it was in 1999, before the cloud was supported by infrastructure and standards. Andreessen was nearly starting from scratch with the concept. He aimed to sell software as a service, not as a product.

Andreessen speaks at the PC Expo in New York City in June of 1999. At the time, he was preparing to leave AOL and launch Loudcloud.

Loudcloud didn't invent the use of "cloud" in reference to information stored remotely. The term already existed in the telecommunications industry. A person making a telephone call using a landline didn't have to worry about routing or paying for each individual call—it was all handled in the cloud. Andreessen and his Loudcloud cofounders wanted to apply the concept to a computing platform.

Andreessen envisioned Loudcloud as a web hosting company. It would put companies' websites online and maintain them. Unlike other similar services, however, Loudcloud would keep the sites running smoothly with automated software that would provide security, manage web traffic, prevent the site from crashing, and much more. Clients would also be able to choose service packages such as databases, applications, e-mail, and payment systems. The founders called this software Opsware.

Loudcloud was incorporated in September of 1999 at the height of the dot-com boom. The venture capital company Benchmark Capital readily agreed to make a $15 million investment, and the bank Morgan Stanley provided $45 million in financing in 2000. Loudcloud began hiring employees and booking contracts. The company quickly required more space and moved twice to bigger facilities. Andreessen's formal job title was chairman.

The business was turning out to be a success, but then the dot-com bubble burst. Many of Loudcloud's

THE DOT-COM BUBBLE

Netscape was the first Internet company to soar to nearly instant success and prominence. Subsequently, venture capitalists and investors saw the tech sector as an exciting new way to get rich. They poured money into Internet companies with no sound business plans and scant profits. The period from about 1997 to 2000 is now called the dot-com bubble. A speculative bubble occurs when the prices of an asset—such as technology stocks—increase to levels significantly above their real economic value. During the dot-com bubble, the value of the tech-heavy NASDAQ stock exchange quintupled from about 1,000 in 1995 to more than 5,000 in 2000.

Speculative bubbles eventually pop when prices plummet, triggering painful economic consequences. The dot-com bubble began to burst in early 2000 and the NASDAQ began a slide that ended with its value nearly down to 1,100. About half of the new Internet companies failed. Investors lost trillions of dollars. Ultimately, the crash contributed to the American economy falling into a recession.

customers were affected by the crash. Loudcloud had focused on growing fast, and it had spent much of its cash. The company managed to raise an additional $120 million, but then it missed its sales forecast for 2000, booking only $37 million from clients rather than the targeted $100 million. Some of Loudcloud's competitors began going bankrupt. Strapped for money, Loudcloud was unable to find any more investors. Although the company had a solid list of customers, it could not show any profits.

Out of options, cofounder and CEO Ben Horowitz decided to take the company public. The timing was terrible since tech companies were drastically losing value on the stock market. Andreessen traveled with other Loudcloud executives across the country to give presentations on Loudcloud to potential investors, who were generally wary of putting money into the tech sector. Halfway through the trip, economic conditions forced the company to reduce the proposed price per share. A week before the scheduled IPO, Steve Hamm of *Businessweek* magazine published an article describing it as the "IPO from hell." In the end, the IPO succeeded in raising the necessary money to continue building the business, although the final stock price barely met expectations. Earlier in the year, the company had held an estimated value of more than $1 billion. After the IPO, the figure was reduced to less than half a billion.

TRANSFORMATION TO OPSWARE

Throughout 2001, the turbulent economic conditions in the tech sector continued to impact Loudcloud's business. Sales prospects declined as the companies who paid for Loudcloud's services struggled. Loudcloud was forced to reduce its earnings forecast for the year—a troubling move for a company recently gone public. Fifteen percent of the company's six hundred employees were laid off. Money was running out again. Loudcloud's executives began to realize that the company could go bankrupt.

Even as Loudcloud struggled, Andreessen himself was still prominent enough to be featured as keynote speaker at the 2001 Oracle Open World conference.

Loudcloud's founders decided to split the company into two separate entities: the web hosting service Loudcloud and the software business Opsware. The company was making its money with the web hosting, but Opsware comprised its intellectual property. Andreessen believed that the software component was more likely to survive in the bleak market conditions. Loudcloud arranged to sell its web hosting business to the Internet services company Electronic Data Systems Corporation (EDS) for $63.5 million.

With the split, the company, now rebranded as Opsware, lost all of its customers and revenue. Opsware had fewer than one hundred employees—some of the original Loudcloud employees moved to EDS while others lost their jobs. The price of Opsware stock fell to $0.35 per share. The company scrambled to adapt products for the market.

EDS was Opsware's first client. The company had agreed to license Opsware's software as part of the Loudcloud sale. After less than a year, though, EDS announced that it was dissatisfied with Opsware's performance and wanted to cancel the contract. Losing its biggest customer would lead to bankruptcy. In 2004, to appease EDS, Opsware acquired a small company called Tangram in order to include a specific piece of software in their EDS package. Opsware managed to keep the EDS account, and Tangram proved to be a useful acquisition.

By transforming Loudcloud into Opsware, Andreessen demonstrated his knack for recognizing niches for tech products in a continually evolving market.

BEN HOROWITZ

Ben Horowitz (1966–) has known Marc Andreessen since his stint as a product manager at Netscape in 1995. Horowitz studied computer science in college and started his career as an engineer at SGI. During his time at Netscape, he was quickly promoted and chose to stay with the company even when it began to struggle and he could have found work elsewhere. After Netscape was acquired by AOL in 1998, Horowitz led its e-commerce

Loudcloud cofounder and CEO Ben Horowitz attributes Opsware's eventual success to aggressive investment in a quality product despite tough economic conditions.

division. He joined two other former Netscape colleagues to found Loudcloud with Andreessen.

Horowitz considers Andreessen a friend as well as a business partner. Today, they continue to work together as the founders of the Andreessen-Horowitz venture capital firm, established in 2009. In 2014, Horowitz published a business advice book, *The Hard Thing About Hard Things: Building a Business When There Are No Easy Answers,* in which he tackles subjects from demoting a friend to developing a CEO skill set.

Over the next few years, Opsware succeeded in broadening its product line, gaining customers, and increasing the value of its stock. Andreessen, however, began to take a less active role in the company. He was focusing on starting up another new company, Ning.

As Opsware began to make solid profits, larger companies showed interest in acquiring it. In July of 2007, Andreessen announced on his blog, "HP buys my company Opsware for more than $1.6 billion in cash." The information technology giant Hewlett-Packard was acquiring Opsware for $14.25 per share.

Andreessen, who owned nearly 10 percent of the company, made more than $100 million on the sale. The deal also put him on the elite list of people who had founded two $1 billion dollar companies. Eventually, many former Opsware employees would join the Andreessen Horowitz venture capital firm.

In 2009, Andreessen was elected to the board of directors of HP. He became an influential figure on a board that was notorious for its disagreements and upheavals.

Looking back at his Opsware experience, Andreessen later stated that the company had been five or six years ahead of its time. After the dot-com crash, economic conditions in the tech sector gradually recovered. Technological advances, such as cheaper servers and the development of innovative software technology, have made cloud computing today much easier and more convenient than back in 1999 when Andreessen debuted one of the first cloud companies.

Chapter Five

STAYING CONNECTED WITH SOCIAL MEDIA

A year or so after founding Facebook in 2004, Mark Zuckerberg had a question for Marc Andreessen, now a Silicon Valley veteran. Zuckerberg wondered, what did Netscape do?

Like Andreessen, Zuckerberg launched an innovative and highly successful company at a young age. But Zuckerberg came from a different generation. Unlike Andreessen, Zuckerberg couldn't remember the days before the Internet. The browser wars were over, with Netscape in decline, by the time he started programming. He'd heard of Netscape but didn't know anything about it.

The rise of Zuckerberg and a new wave of tech entrepreneurs represented a shifting trend on the Internet. If the early days of the web had been about distributing information, this new focus was on connection and collaboration. People had become accustomed to constantly being connected by e-mail and cell phones. Now, the most successful new ventures give users the opportunity to share, participate, and network. Social media quickly became widespread. And Andreessen, with his knack for recognizing emerging trends, recognized its potential early on.

Andreessen and Laura Arrillaga-Andreessen chat with Mark Zuckerberg at the 2012 Allen & Company Sun Valley Conference.

GOING SOCIAL

In the first decade of the twenty-first century, with Facebook at the forefront, the Internet went social. In the early days of the web, people were wary about putting personal details online. Eventually, people became comfortable with disclosing their real names and other details

of their lives. They went to the web to share their experiences, anecdotes, opinions, and images. The Internet allowed people to stay connected with those from their everyday lives and build up new online communities of friends across the world. Social media sites sprang up that provided tools to facilitate sharing content across communities and networks.

This new phase of the Internet—the social media–dominated resurgence of new services after the dot-com crash—

has sometimes been dubbed Web 2.0. The term refers to how people use online resources rather than any technological change. Andreessen attended a couple of the Web 2.0 Conferences that were held from 2004 onward, organized by O'Reilly Media, to discuss the next generation of Internet advances. He was skeptical of the idea that Web 2.0 was a technological turning point. He thought that the web was merely evolving as a medium and that "Web 2.0" was just a buzzword that would quickly become outdated. Nonetheless, he recognized the possibilities opened up by social media before it became ubiquitous, or ever-present, in both the public sphere and our personal lives.

Social networking has a lot to offer: It gives people connectivity, convenience, a means of entertainment, and an easy way to share knowledge. It offers organizations and businesses new means of communicating with the public. Social media applications have proven valuable in health, education, law enforcement, activism, and many other spheres. But social media has also been criticized for invasion of personal privacy and diminishing people's engagement with the real world. Regardless of the overall pros and cons, social media has become entrenched in contemporary society, and it will continue to advance with new services as well as new means of keeping people connected.

INTRODUCING NING

In 2004, Andreessen started the platform Ning, a social networking company, with cofounder Gina Bianchini. She was an experienced Silicon Valley entrepreneur who had previously started Harmonic Communications, a company that sold software for Internet advertising. Although it was an innovative concept, the dot-com crash wiped out the market for her products. Nonetheless, she managed to convince Andreessen that there was still a bright future in Internet ventures, and the biggest trends were in social media. Andreessen held the position of chief technology officer at Ning, and Bianchini was CEO of the company. Ning launched in October of 2005.

Ning was based on the concept of do-it-yourself social apps that could be used by groups. According to *Fortune* magazine, Andreessen developed Ning with the idea in mind that "people will move narrow aspects of their social lives onto the Net, convening online in groups specifically for, say, beagle owners." The platform would allow users without any programming expertise to design their own apps using web services. Much like blogging provided people with a template for publishing their views, Ning would give people the basic tools for creating their own niche social networks. Users could share photos, messages, or reviews, for example, using an app with customized features and designs.

In addition to serving as chief technology officer, Andreessen personally invested $9 million in Ning, making him the company's primary backer.

The service would be free for members. The company would make money by selling advertising as well as extra tools and features.

By now, Andreessen was savvy about finding backers for his projects. Over the course of the next few years, he raised nearly $120 million from venture capital firms and other investors. In mid-2009, the company was valued at $750 million. Ning moved into offices that had once been occupied by Facebook.

In March of 2010, Bianchini stepped down from her CEO position to join the Andreessen Horowitz venture capital firm. Ning had grown to 2.3 million networks consisting of 45 million members; the company's highest-profile customer was the rapper 50 Cent. The new CEO, Jason Rosenthal, had been an employee of Andreessen's at Netscape, Loudcloud, and Opsware, before joining Ning as an executive.

A month later, Rosenthal announced that Ning would no longer function as a free service. Its user networks would either pay or be shut down. The company also downsized its staff from 167 to 98 people. Over the next year, the number of paying members increased, as did Ning's revenue.

In September 2011, Andreessen announced that Ning—which now had more than one hundred thousand networks—was being acquired by Glam Media (renamed Mode Media in 2014), a social content platform. Its price was estimated to be $200 million—far less than the 2009 valuation. Andreessen joined the Glam Media board of directors, a position he still holds.

Years later, in describing Ning to Tad Friend of *The New Yorker* magazine, Andreessen would say, "It didn't do great." He has also stated that in 2004—when even Facebook was not yet available to the general public—the concept of social media apps was ahead of its time.

BRANCHING OUT

Andreessen sometimes speaks of a mental generational divide between Silicon Valley entrepreneurs such as himself who experienced the dot-com crash firsthand and those who arrived afterward. He has said many times that he feels that he still carries scars from watching the crisis wreak havoc on the tech industry. Nevertheless, even in the after-

math of the crash, as many Silicon Valley figures were pessimistic about the Internet's prospects, incredible tech advances continued. Broadband access became wide-spread, the first smartphones were released, social media began to evolve, and Wi-Fi entered the mainstream.

Today, after observing and participating in the ups and downs of the sector for more than two decades,

Andreessen and Jason Rosenthal prepare to give an interview in February 2011. Ning saw solid revenue gains in the year after Rosenthal became CEO.

Andreessen remains an optimist about technology's transformative potential. He once told Kevin Roose of *New York* magazine that "My presumptive tendency, when I'm presented with a new idea, is not to ask, 'Is it going to work?' It's, 'Well, what if it does work?'" He believes that technological advances will continue to bring about dramatic improvements in people's daily lives and in society at large and that technology has the potential to solve many of the problems in sectors such as education and health care. From the perspective of a Silicon Valley insider, Andreessen is constantly seeing innovative plans being developed by start-ups. He has great respect for young would-be entrepreneurs with big ideas, especially those who are interested in founding and running their own companies as CEOs. Some of the most successful tech companies were built by founder-CEOs, including Apple, Facebook, Microsoft, and Amazon.

Even as he continued his involvement in Ning, Andreessen began to branch out. He made investments

OUR ROBOT FUTURE

Marc Andreessen believes in a vision of the future in which everyone in the world will have access to the Internet, everyone will use cloud computing, and robots and artificial intelligence (AI) will be part of our daily lives. In an interview with *CTOvision*, for example, Andreessen discussed possible ways that technology of the future will change how people drive. Self-driving cars may become widespread. In cars still driven by humans, sensors could be installed to detect whether a person is driving unsafely. A car could alert destinations about its imminent arrival. These features could be convenient and beneficial to society, but they also raise issues about privacy and civil liberties. Similar questions apply to many other areas that could be affected by AI and robotics.

Andreessen has also addressed the issue of whether computers and other technological advances are displacing humans in the labor force and costing jobs. He acknowledges that technological change transforms the way that people live and work but believes that economic conditions will open up new opportunities. On his blog, he wrote that "there is still an enormous gap between what many people do in jobs today, and what robots and AI can replace. And there will be for decades."

In 2013, the venture capital firm Andreessen Horowitz invested in Anki, which Andreessen praised as the best robotics start-up he'd seen. The company boasts on its website, "We're building on decades of scientific research to make artificial intelligence accessible to everyone. We are dedicated to bringing consumer robotics into everyday life." So far, however, its sole product is a racing game for toy cars.

in promising start-ups as well as in larger companies that he considered to have a good likelihood of expanding and becoming giants in the sector. Many of these have involved social networking. A few of the companies Andreessen invested in include LinkedIn, a social network for business professionals, Digg, the news source for the most talked-about stories on the Internet, Twitter, the microblog site, Instagram, the photo and video sharing service acquired by Facebook in 2012, and Rockmelt, a company that aimed to create a social media–oriented web browser.

Andreessen has long been involved in Facebook, as an advisor to Zuckerberg as well as an investor. In 2006, he urged Zuckerberg to refuse an offer by the tech giant Yahoo! to buy Facebook for $1 billion. The recommendation proved savvy because Facebook was worth around $245 billion in June 2015. Andreessen invested in Facebook early on, and later, Andreessen Horowitz invested heavily in Facebook as well as Twitter. In 2008, Andreessen joined the board of Facebook, a position he still holds.

Andreessen has also been involved in a wide variety of tech ventures unrelated to social media. From 2008 to 2014, he sat on the board of eBay, the online auction site. As mentioned earlier, he is a member of the board of HP. Andreessen has also invested in media companies such as Buzzfeed and *Business Insider,* which includes the notice "Disclosure: Marc Andreessen is an investor

By 2013, Andreessen was a veteran Silicon Valley insider, well positioned to advise and support young tech entrepreneurs with big ideas for the future.

in *Business Insider*," on the page of any news story that mentions Andreessen. He also sits on the boards of many smaller companies that he or Andreessen Horowitz has invested in.

When he began investing, Andreessen started out by putting $25,000 to $100,000 in a company, which is considered a small investment. This made him an angel investor—a wealthy individual who invests money in a company, usually early in its existence, in return for an ownership stake or other interest. Many of Andreessen's investments were made in partnership with his long-time colleague Ben Horowitz. Together, the pair became known as super-angel investors for their connections and high level of investment in a variety of companies.

Chapter Six

ENTREPRENEURSHIP AND THE NEXT BIG THINGS

With his expertise in managing technology companies and extensive connections in the tech world, Marc Andreessen was well positioned to focus on investing and helping advance the next generation of entrepreneurs. In 2009, he formed the venture capital firm known as Andreessen Horowitz with colleague and fellow investor Ben Horowitz. It is sometimes abbreviated "a16z" because there are sixteen letters between the beginning "A" of Andreessen and the final "z" of Horowitz—the firm's website is http://a16z.com.

In general, Andreessen Horowitz maintains a policy of investing in companies involved in information technology, mostly American and mostly in Silicon Valley. They believe that there are still plenty of innovative

concepts yet to come that could trigger dramatic trans-
formations in computing. The firm looks for companies
that are idealistic about their product's potential yet also
pragmatic about its likelihood to succeed. As Andreessen told *The New Yorker*'s Tad Friend in 2015, "We're not
funding Mother Teresa. We're funding imperial, will-
to-power people who want to crush their competition.
Companies can only have
a big impact on the world
if they get big."

ANDREESSEN HOROWITZ, VENTURE CAPITAL FIRM

Investing through a ven-
ture capital firm is gen-
erally very different from
angel investing. Although
venture capital firms maintain a high profile in the
tech sector, angel investors
actually fund a larger total
number of start-ups with
smaller amounts of money.
Angel investors risk their

own money, while investors working for venture capital firms largely invest the money of financial institutions and other funds. An "angel round" of investing is likely to take place in the early stages of a company's development. The "venture capital round" typically takes place slightly later, when the company has solid potential for high growth. Typically, angel investors are more likely to care

Andreessen attends the 2012 Wired Business Conference in Partnership with MDC Partners, which focused on the disruptive forces of technology in business.

about the success of the company, while venture capital-ists focus on the return they will get on the investment in the end. A venture capital firm is highly structured, with a small number of general partners making the key deci-sions concerning investments. Venture capitalists have a reputation for providing mentorship to young company executives as well as demanding a certain amount of con-trol to protect their investment. They reap the returns of the investment by selling their stake once the company is well established, often when it goes public or is sold to a larger company. For both angel investors and venture capitalists, start-ups are considered risky investments, and less than half of all start-ups go on to succeed.

From the beginning, Andreessen Horowitz intended to employ more flexibility in setting up deals than traditional venture capital firms. Many firms exclu-sively provide minimum amounts in the millions, which requires a long, complex process to come to an agreement with the company. Andreessen Horowitz planned to act as angel investors to some companies when appropriate. In Andreessen's view, the conventional venture capital approach hasn't kept up with changing business models. Today, companies starting up don't always establish a for-mal hierarchy, and it's easier than in the past for them to develop a marketable product without a large workforce or a significant early investment. To Andreessen Horow-itz, angel round investing benefits the venture capital

A MODEL ON TALENT

Andreessen Horowitz has also set itself apart by modeling its approach on a Hollywood talent agency. Rather than employing a minimal support staff, like many venture capital firms, Andreessen Horowitz has more than fifty employees in market development, technical talent, executive talent, marketing, and corporate development. Among its special advisors is economist Lawrence Summers, who is the former secretary of

Renowned economist Lawrence Summers has held numerous high-profile positions during his long career, both in public service and in the private sector.

the U.S. Treasury, president of Harvard University, and director of the National Economic Council. Andreessen Horowitz provides its entrepreneurs with services, connections, and advice. It also aggressively recruits promising companies, sometimes bidding against rival investors. The firm has sometimes been accused of driving up valuations of these companies and even contributing to a bubble by creating artificially high prices.

firm and the entrepreneurs at the start-up. It does invest millions or even tens of millions in established companies, but it also invests smaller amounts, even as little as $50,000, to give a boost to promising start-ups.

Andreessen Horowitz started out in 2009 by raising $300 million for investments. At the time, observers were interested in watching how the two well-connected angel investors would fare when they turned to investing as venture capitalists. Almost immediately, Andreessen Horowitz made headlines by investing $50 million in the Internet telecommunications company Skype, then valued at $2.75 billion—it had been assumed that the firm would start out with smaller, safer buys. In 2011, Microsoft acquired Skype for $8.7 billion, making Andreessen Horowitz's share worth $153 million. The firm has continued to grow, and in 2015, it managed more than $4 billion in assets.

Andreessen Horowitz invests in fifteen companies a year. Today, the firm has a portfolio of nearly one hundred companies. A handful of the names are well-known. The firm has paid $130 million for shares of Facebook and Twitter and also has investments in the online home and room rental service Airbnb, the local search service Foursquare, and Pinterest, the media collection and display site. Some of Andreessen Horowitz's more futuristic-leaning investments include Oculus, a virtual reality headset company; Jawbone, a wearable technology company; Soylent, the food substitute company; and Coinbase, a virtual wallet for the digital currency bitcoin. Andreessen sits on the boards of several of the companies in Andreessen Horowitz's portfolio, including the mobile game company TinyCo, the robotics company Anki, and Samsara, which makes sensors for networks. Investments made in 2015 include Stack Exchange, a network of question and answer sites, and Distelli, a software as a service company.

The two cofounders complement each other as a team in terms of their personalities and strengths that they bring to the firm. Andreessen is the visionary and theorist. Horowitz is the skilled manager who is good at dealing with people—Andreessen has even said that he doesn't really like people. Nonetheless, Andreessen's enthusiasm for innovation hasn't invariably led to successful deals. He's sometimes been accused of valuing companies too high, leading to lower returns on the investment or even substantial losses.

THE TWEETSTORMER

Andreessen possesses a wide range of knowledge and has an opinion to express on every issue, often a strong or even controversial opinion. He's interested in political issues, societal trends, history, philosophy, science, philanthropy, pop culture, and, above all, technology and economics, especially the nuts-and-bolts matters of starting up and running a company.

Andreessen is often happy to speak at length to interviewers. A *Financial Times* reporter noted that the transcript of her lunchtime conversation with Andreessen amounted to nearly twenty thousand words—the length of a short novella. He sometimes provokes jour-

A user demonstrates Jawbone's UP24 fitness tracker, displaying data on an iPhone, at the Wearable Expo in Tokyo, Japan, in 2015.

nalists with his views on the news business, recommending frequently that newspapers discontinue their print versions and concentrate on digital. Andreessen is savvy at generating publicity for his ventures and causes. He was the public face of Netscape and Opsware, and now he is the most high-profile and outspoken member of Andreessen Horowitz.

During 2007 and 2008, Andreessen maintained a blog that became highly popular for its frank commentary on financial matters and current events during the recession. It included the "Pmarca Guide to Startups" and "The truth about venture capitalists" series of posts. Since 2009, when he started Andreessen Horowitz, he has published occasional business-related posts.

Some of Andreessen's opinion pieces have spurred controversy and discussion. In 2011, he

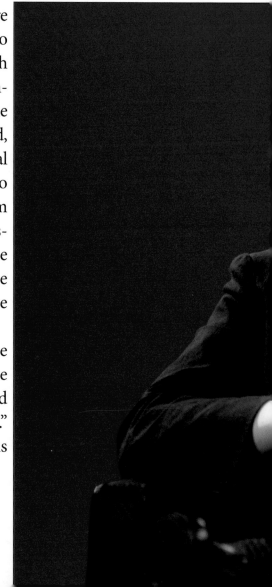

wrote an essay for the *Wall Street Journal* called "Why Software Is Eating the World." He predicted that software companies would disrupt many economic sectors by providing online services. He gave the example of the transformation of the publishing industry, the music industry, photography, and movie services, pointing out that the most influential companies in each are actually software companies. Andreessen predicted that the software industry would continue to grow and defended the high valuations of some companies. His points in the essay were widely debated, prompting the influential magazine *The Economist* to publish a profile of the firm titled, "Disrupting the Disrupters." Today, the phrase "Software Is Eating the World" is featured on the a16z.com site.

In early 2014, he wrote a guest article for the *New York Times* entitled "Why Bitcoin Matters." He's impressed by bitcoins as a technical breakthrough in computer science, and he believes that businesses as well as consumers should be impressed by its potential for limiting credit card fraud and transaction fees. In addition, Andreessen Horowitz has invested $50 million in bitcoin-related companies.

Also in 2014, Andreessen revisited the topic of computers displacing human labor in a blog post titled

Andreessen speaks at the 2013 Uplinq Mobile Developers Conference 2013, an event focusing on the technical and business potential of mobile devices.

"This is Probably a Good Time to Say That I Don't Believe Robots Will Eat All the Jobs." He argued that technological change is beneficial for society at large even when it does cost some jobs and that the future will hold new fields and new jobs that we can't even imagine today.

In 2014, Andreessen revived his long-dormant Twitter account where he tweets as @pmarca, which stands for "private Marc A." He quickly became known as a prolific and opinionated Twitter user. Andreessen has said that he views Twitter as an ideal means of publicizing his thoughts to the public and the media. He typically averages about one hundred tweets a day—some are retweets or quotes—and he composes all of his personal tweets himself. He's become notorious for tweetstorms, which

LAURA ARRILLAGA-ANDREESSEN

Laura Arrillaga-Andreessen (1970–) is a prominent Silicon Valley philanthropist who lectures on philanthropy at Stanford University. She met Marc Andreessen at a New Year's Eve dinner in 2005, and she knew that she wanted to get to know him better because "he was a genius, he was a coder, he was funny, and he was bald," as she told Tad Friend of *The New Yorker*. She also asked him about his philanthropic work.

Arrillaga-Andreessen is the daughter of billionaire real estate developer John Arrillaga. She holds undergraduate and graduate degrees from Stanford, including an MBA. She is president of the Laura Arrillaga-Andreessen Foundation and the Marc and Laura Andreessen Foundation, and she is involved with many other institutions and philanthropic organizations, including the venture philanthropy fund Silicon Valley Social Venture Fund (SV2), which she founded. In 2011, she published *Giving 2.0: Transform Your Giving and Our World.* Arrillaga-Andreessen advises other Silicon Valley entrepreneurs on their philanthropic giving. For example, she advised Facebook founder Mark Zuckerberg before he gave $100 million to Newark Public Schools.

Laura Arrillaga-Andreessen speaks on "A New Vision for Philanthropy" at the 2014 Vanity Fair New Establishment Summit, themed "The Age of Innovation."

are Twitter lectures in the form of a series of numbered posts, usually on tech, investing, and economics topics. For example, at 11:33 a.m. on January 5, 2015, Andreessen continued his bitcoin analysis with "1/Some thoughts on the state of Bitcoin, cryptocurrencies, and distributed transaction and trust networks at start of 2015!" By 12:01 p.m., he'd reached his conclusion, with "25/ What to watch in 2015: New apps, new use cases, international adoption, consumer education, technological innovation & spinoff ideas!"

PRIVACY AND LEGACY

In 2006, Andreessen married Silicon Valley socialite and philanthropist Laura Arrillaga. Andreessen is apparently estranged from his family back in Wisconsin—the notoriously private man does not discuss this matter with reporters—and nobody from his family attended the wedding. In 2014, the couple welcomed their first child, a son, into the world. They named the boy John for Arrillaga-Andreessen's father.

Andreessen and Arrillaga-Andreessen consider

Andreessen has stated that when he asked Laura Arrillaga to be his steady girlfriend, he made a pitch that sounded like a start-up founder's spiel to an investor.

87

themselves homebodies. On the bio page of her LAAF. org site, Arrillaga-Andreessen mentions that she and Andreessen "enjoy reading, art, writing, movies, athletics, sleeping, not sleeping and laughing as much as possible." Andreessen, who was once chubby and known for enjoying cookies and hamburgers in his Netscape days, now exercises and eats a healthy diet. Nonetheless, he's still a regular at a couple of diners near his home in Palo Alto, where he often holds meetings. He's said that he enjoyed the TV show *Silicon Valley,* which satirizes, or mocks, his home base.

According to *Forbes,* Andreessen's net worth (his wealth after taxes) is $600 million. In 2015, he was ranked nineteenth on the magazine's "Midas List" of venture capitalists.

Andreessen and Arrillaga-Andreessen have been putting some of their wealth and influence toward good causes. In 2007, the couple gave a $27.5 million donation to Stanford Hospital's emergency department. In 2012, he announced on his blog that the partners at Andreessen Horowitz were pledging to give half of their income from venture capital to charity during their lifetimes.

In 2013, Andreessen was awarded the Queen Elizabeth Prize for Engineering. On his blog, he acknowledged Eric Bina and the NCSA team for their contributions to Mosaic.

Andreessen avoids talking about his legacy or the contributions he still hopes to achieve. Even when discussing Andreessen Horowitz's success, he cautions that it will take ten or fifteen years to prove the firm's ranking among other Silicon Valley firms. But he takes a characteristically more optimistic view of the general future of technology in the conclusion of a 2014 tweetstorm: "12/ Assumption *must* be: Tech entrepreneurship all over the world is going to expand a thousand fold in the next 20 years. How could it not?"

Timeline

July 9, 1971 Marc Andreessen is born.

September 1989 Andreessen starts college at the University of Illinois.

January 1992 Andreessen starts working at the National Center for Supercomputing Applications (NCSA).

January 23, 1993 Andreessen releases the web browser NCSA Mosaic.

January 1994 Andreessen moves to California to work for Enterprise Integration Technologies, Inc.

April 1994 Andreessen and Jim Clark start up Mosaic Communications (later known as Netscape Communications Corporation).

October 13, 1994 Mosaic Netscape 0.9 is launched.

December 15, 1994 Netscape Navigator 1.0 is released.

August 9, 1995 Netscape goes public with its IPO.

December 1995 The value of Netscape is at $171 per share.

February 1996 Andreessen is featured on the cover of *Time* magazine.

November 1998 Netscape is acquired by AOL; Andreessen becomes AOL's chief technology officer.

September 1999 Andreessen leaves AOL and founds Loudcloud.

2001 The dot-com bubble bursts.

September 2002 Loudcloud is rebranded as Opsware, a software company.

September 2004 Andreessen founds the networking company Ning.

2006 Andreessen marries Laura Arrillaga.

July 2007 Hewlett-Packard acquires Opsware for $1.6 billion.

November 2007 Andreessen and Arrillaga-Andreessen donate $27.5 million to Stanford Hospital's emergency department.

2008 AOL abandons the Navigator browser.

July 2009 Andreessen founds Andreessen Horowitz with Ben Horowitz.

September 2009 Andreessen Horowitz invests $50 million in Skype.

Andreessen joins the board of directors for HP.

May 2011 Microsoft acquires Skype for $8.7 billion.

August 2011 Andreessen publishes the article "Why Software Is Eating the World."

September 2011 Ning is acquired by Glam Media.

March 2013 Andreessen is awarded the Queen Elizabeth Prize for Engineering.

Glossary

acquisition The obtaining of ownership or a controlling interest in a company.

anticompetitive Likely to prevent or restrain competition.

antitrust Regulating or opposing trusts and other business monopolies, especially to promote fair competition.

broadband A type of connection to the Internet that allows users to send or receive a lot of information very quickly.

code Instructions for computer programming.

dot-com bubble The stock market bubble that inflated the value of Internet firms in the late 1990s; many of these collapsed when the bubble popped in 2001.

entrepreneur An individual who organizes and operates a business, especially one that involves a financial risk.

hypertext A computer system that lets users move to new information by clicking on highlighted text.

infrastructure The basic features or structure of a system or organization.

initial public offering (IPO) A private company's first sale of stock to the public.

interface Hardware or software that enables communication between a computer and user.

investor A person who puts money into an enterprise, such as a corporation, with the expectation of financial returns and eventually generating a profit.

license To grant formal permission to enter or use the property of another, such as a patent or copyright.

open source The term used for software for which the original source code is free and open to be modified and redistributed.

philanthropy The practice of donating money to humanitarian causes.

platform The model for a computer's hardware system, which directs the types of software it is able to run.

private sector The section of the economy that is run by individuals or groups, not by the government.

programmer A person who writes computer code for software.

server A computer that controls or performs certain tasks for other computers in a network.

venture capitalist A private investor or investment firm that provides money to a new or expanding company, often high-tech, with the expectation of a high return because of high risk.

For More Information

Andreessen Horowitz
2865 Sand Hill Road, Suite 101
Menlo Park, CA 94025
Website: http://a16z.com/
Andreessen Horowitz is the venture capital firm
    founded by Marc Andreessen and Ben Horowitz.

Computer History Museum
1401 N. Shoreline Boulevard
Mountain View, CA 94043
(650) 810-1010
Website: http://www.computerhistory.org
The museum seeks to preserve and present for
    posterity information age artifacts and stories.

MediaSmarts
950 Gladstone Avenue, Suite 120
Ottawa, ON K1Y 3E6
Canada
(613) 224-7721
Website: http://mediasmarts.ca/
MediaSmarts is Canada's center for digital and
    media literacy.

National Science Foundation
4201 Wilson Boulevard
Arlington, VA 22230
(703) 292-5111
Website: http://www.nsf.gov/
The NSF is a government agency that funds scientific research in a variety of fields.

Startup Canada
116 Lisgar Street, Suite 300
Ottawa, ON K2P 0C2
Canada
(613) 627-0787
Website: http://www.startupcan.ca/
Startup Canada is made up of entrepreneurs who work
to build entrepreneurial growth and success.

WEBSITES

Because of the changing nature of Internet links, Rosen Publishing has developed an online list of websites related to the subject
of this book. This site is updated regularly. Please use this link to
access the list: http://www.rosenlinks.com/TP/And

For Further Reading

Arrillaga-Andreessen, Laura. *Giving 2.0: Transform Your Giving and Our World.* San Francisco, CA: Jossey-Bass, 2011.

Bilton, Nick. *Hatching Twitter: A True Story of Money, Power, Friendship, and Betrayal.* New York, NY: Penguin, 2014.

Blank, Steve, and Bob Dorf. *The Startup Owner's Manual: The Step-By-Step Guide for Building a Great Company.* Pescadero, CA: K&S Ranch Press, 2012.

Brasch, Nicholas. *The Technology Behind the Internet.* Mankato, MN: Smart Apple Media, 2011.

Brockman, John, ed. *Is the Internet Changing the Way You Think? The Net's Impact on Our Minds and Future.* New York, NY: Harper Perennial, 2011.

Draper, William H. *The Startup Game: Inside the Partnership between Venture Capitalists and Entrepreneurs.* New York, NY: Palgrave Macmillan, 2011.

Feld, Brad, and Jason Mendelson. *Venture Deals: Be Smarter Than Your Lawyer and Venture Capitalist.* Hoboken, NJ: John Wiley and Sons, Inc., 2012.

Ford, Martin. *Rise of the Robots: Technology and the Threat of a Jobless Future.* New York, NY: Basic Books, 2015.

Frauenfelder, Mark. *The Computer: An Illustrated History From Its Origins to the Present Day.* New York, NY: Carlton Books, 2013.

Goldsmith, Mike. *Computer.* New York, NY: DK Publishing, 2011.

Henderson, Harry. *The Digital Age.* San Diego, CA: ReferencePoint Books, 2013.

Isaacson, Walter. *The Innovators: How a Group of Hackers, Geniuses, and Geeks Created the Digital Revolution.* New York, NY: Simon and Schuster, 2014.

Kallen, Stuart A. *The Information Revolution.* San Diego, CA: Lucent Books, 2010.

Karam, Andrew. *Artificial Intelligence.* New York, NY: Chelsea House/Infobase Learning, 2012.

Kirkpatrick, David. *The Facebook Effect: The Inside Story of the Company That Is Connecting the World.* New York, NY: Simon & Schuster, 2011.

Levy, Steven. *Hackers: Heroes of the Computer Revolution.* Sebastopol, CA: O'Reilly Media, 2010.

Lewis, Michael. *The New New Thing: A Silicon Valley*

Story. New York, NY: W. W. Norton & Company, 2014.

Marcovitz, Hal. *Online Information and Research.* San Diego, CA: ReferencePoint Press, 2012.

McDowell, Gayle Laakmann. *The Google Resume: How to Prepare for a Career and Land a Job at Apple, Microsoft, Google, or any Top Tech Company.* Hoboken, NJ: Wiley, 2011.

Popper, Nathaniel. *Digital Gold: Bitcoin and the Inside Story of the Misfits and Millionaires Trying to Reinvent Money.* New York, NY: HarperCollins, 2015.

Szumski, Bonnie. *How Are Online Activities Affecting Society?* (In Controversy). San Diego, CA: ReferencePoint Press, 2013.

Thiel, Peter, with Blake Masters. *Zero to One: Notes on Startups, or How to Build the Future.* New York, NY: Crown Business, 2014.

Willard, Nancy. *Cyber Savvy: Embracing Digital Safety and Civility.* Newbury Park, CA: Corwin, 2011.

Yoffie, David B., and Michael A. Cusumano. *Strategy Rules: Five Timeless Lessons from Bill Gates, Andy Grove, and Steve Jobs.* New York, NY: HarperCollins, 2015.

Bibliography

Anderson, Chris. "The Man Who Makes the Future: Wired Icon Marc Andreessen." Wired, April 24, 2012. Retrieved June 5, 2015 (http://www.wired .com/2012/04/ff_andreessen/all/).

Andreessen, Marc. "An Update from Ning Chairman & Co-Founder Marc Andreessen." Ning.com, March 15, 2010. Retrieved June 5, 2015 (http://www.ning.com/ blog/2010/03/an-update-from-ning-chairman-co-founder-marc-andreessen.html).

Andreessen, Marc. "Marc Andreessen, General Partner at Andreessen Horowitz." LinkedIn.com. Retrieved June 5, 2015 (https://www.linkedin.com/in/pmarca).

Andreessen, Marc. "Marc Andreessen — @pmarca." Tweet-storm.io. Retrieved June 5, 2015 (http://tweetstorm.io/ user/pmarca).

Andreessen, Marc. "pmarca-archive: An Archive of Classic Marc Andreessen Blog Posts." Retrieved June 5, 2015 (http://blog.jedchristiansen.com/pmarcaarchive/ welcome-2800/).

Andreessen, Marc. "This is Probably a Good Time to Say That I Don't Believe Robots Will Eat All the Jobs…" June 13, 2014. Retrieved June 5, 2015 (http://blog.pmarca. com/2014/06/13/this-is-probably-a-good-time-to-say-that-i-dont-believe-robots-will-eat-all-the-jobs/).

Andreessen, Marc. "Why Bitcoin Matters." *New York Times.* January 21, 2014. Retrieved June 5, 2015 (http://dealbook .nytimes.com/2014/01/21/why-bitcoin-matters/).

Andreessen, Marc. "Why Software Is Eating The World." *Wall Street Journal,* August 20, 2011.

Anki.com. "Anki: Company Overview." Anki, 2015. Retrieved June 5, 2015 (https://anki.com/en-us/company).

Austin, Scott. "Microsoft's Skype Buy Delivers More Than Profits To Andreessen Horowitz." *Wall Street Journal,* May 10, 2011. Retrieved June 5, 2015 (http://blogs.wsj.com/venturecapital/2011/05/10/microsofts-skype-buy-delivers-more-than-profits-to-andreessen-horowitz/).

Cailliau, Robert, and James Gillies. *How the Web Was Born.* New York, NY: Oxford University Press, 2000.

Campbell, W. Joseph. *1995: The Year the Future Began.* Oakland, CA: University of California Press, 2015.

Carlyle, Erin. "Marc Andreessen." *Forbes*, September 19, 2012. Retrieved June 5, 2015 (http://www.forbes.com/special-report/2012/forbes-400/ones-to-watch/profiles/0917_ones-to-watch_marc-andreessen.html).

Cassidy, John. *Dot.con: The Greatest Story Ever Sold.* New York, NY: HarperCollins, 2002.

Clark, Jim, and Owen Edwards. *Netscape Time: The Making of the Billion-Dollar Start-Up That Took On Microsoft.* New York, NY: St. Martin's Press, 1999.

Daniel, Caroline. "Lunch with the FT: Marc Andreessen." *Financial Times*, January 16, 2015. Retrieved June 5, 2015 (http://www.ft.com/cms/s/0/a0137c36-9659-11e4-922f-00144feabdc0.html).

Economist, The. "Disrupting the Disrupters." September 3, 2011. Retrieved June 5, 2015 (http://www.economist.com/node/21527020).

Elgin, Ben. "The Last Days of Net Mania." Bloomberg. April 15, 2001. Retrieved June 5, 2015 (http://www.bloomberg.com/bw/stories/2001-04-15/the-last-days-of-net-mania).

Entrepreneur. "Marc Andreessen, Internet Evangelist." *Entrepreneur*, October 9, 2008. Retrieved June 5, 2015 (http://www.entrepreneur.com/article/197600).

Friend, Tad. "Tomorrow's Advance Man: Marc Andreessen's plan to win the future." *New Yorker,* May 18, 2015. Retrieved July 30, 2015 (http://www.newyorker.com/magazine/2015/05/18/tomorrows-advance-man).

Geron, Tomio. "With Revenue Up 400%, Ning Adds Paid Access Service." *Forbes*, June 15, 2011. Retrieved June 5, 2015 (http://www.forbes.com/sites/tomiogeron/2011/06/15/with-revenue-up-400-ning-adds-paid-access-service/).

Gourley, Bob Marc. "Andreessen on the Future of Technology and Implications for Government Service to Citizens." *CTOvision,* May 19, 2014. Retrieved June 5, 2015 (https://ctovision.com/2014/05/marc-andreessen-future-technology-implications-government-service/).

Hamm, Steve. "The Education of Marc Andreessen." *Business Week,* April 2, 1998. Retrieved June 5, 2015 (http://www.businessweek.com/1998/15/topstory.htm).

Horowitz, Ben. *The Hard Thing About Hard Things: Building a Business When There Are No Easy Answers.* New York, NY: HarperCollins, 2015.

Horowitz, Ben. "How Angel Investing Is Different Than Venture Capital." Business Insider, March 2, 2010. Retrieved June 5, 2015 (http://www.businessinsider.com/how-angel-investing-is-different-than-venture-capital-2010-3).

Inside Philanthropy. "Tech Philanthropists: Marc Andreessen." Retrieved June 5, 2015 (http://insidephilanthropy.squarespace.com/guide-to-individual-donors/marc-andreessen.html).

Jacobson, Marc. "EDS Buys Loudcloud Hosting Service." ZDNet, June 21, 2002. Retrieved June 5, 2015 (http://www.zdnet.com/article/eds-buys-loudcloud-hosting-service/).

Jones International and Jones Digital Century. "Marc Andreessen." The History of Computing Project. January 20, 2014. Retrieved June 5, 2015 (http://www.thocp.net/biographies/andreesen_marc.htm).

Kaplan, David A. *The Silicon Boys and Their Valley of Dreams.* New York, NY: William Morrow And Company, Inc., 1999.

Kincaid, Jason. "Ning's Bubble Bursts: No More Free Networks, Cuts 40% Of Staff." TechCrunch, April 15, 2010. Retrieved June 5, 2015 (http://techcrunch.com/2010/04/15/nings-bubble-bursts-no-more-free-networks-cuts-40-of-staff/).

Lacy, Sarah. *Once You're Lucky, Twice You're Good: The Rebirth of Silicon Valley and the Rise of Web 2.0.* New York, NY: Gotham Books, 2008.

Laura Arrillaga-Andreessen Foundation (LAAF). "Laura Arrillaga-Andreessen Biography." Retrieved June 5, 2015 (http://laaf.org/laura-arrillaga-andreessen/).

Maney, Kevin. "Marc Andreessen puts his money where his mouth is." Fortune, July 10, 2009. Retrieved June 5, 2015 (http://archive.fortune.com/2009/07/02/technology/marc_andreessen_venture_fund.fortune/index.htm).

Maney, Kevin. "Marc of the Valley on Newspapers." Wired. October 29, 2008. Retrieved June 5, 2015 (http://www.wired.com/2008/10/marc-of-the-val/).

Markoff, John. "Microsoft vs. Netscape: The Border War Heats Up." *New York Times,* September 29, 1997. Retrieved June 5, 2015 (http://www.nytimes.com/1997/09/29/business/microsoft-vs-netscape-the-border-war-heats-up.html).

Miller, Alaska. "Ning Moves Into Facebook's Old Palo Alto Office." *Business Insider.* November 13, 2009. Retrieved July 30, 2015 (http://www.businessinsider.com/ning-moving-to-facebooks-old-office-2009-11).

Miller, Claire Cain. "Rebooting Philanthropy in Silicon Valley." *New York Times,* December 18, 2011, BU6. Retrieved August 3, 2015 (http://www.nytimes.com/2011/12/18/business/a-philanthropy-reboot-in-silicon-valley.html?_r=0).

Parr, Ben. "Glam Media Acquires Ning." Mashable,

September 20, 2011. Retrieved June 5, 2015 (http://mashable
.com/2011/09/20/glam-media-acquires-ning/).

Primack, Dan. "Brainstorming with Marc Andreessen." *Fortune*, April 10, 2015. Retrieved June 5, 2015 (http://fortune.
com/2015/04/10/brainstorming-with-marc-andreessen/).

Quittner, Joshua, and Michelle Slatalla. *Speeding the Net:
The Inside Story of Netscape and How It Challenged
Microsoft*. New York, NY: Atlantic Monthly Press, 1998.

Roose, Kevin. "Marc Andreessen in Conversation." *New
York*. October 19, 2014. Retrieved June 5, 2015 (http://
nymag.com/daily/intelligencer/2014/10/marc-andreessen-in-conversation.html).

Salmon, Felix. "The Problem with Marc Andreessen." Reuters, April 26, 2012. Retrieved June 5, 2015 (http://blogs
.reuters.com/felix-salmon/2012/04/26/the-problem-with-marc-andreessen/).

Scheiber, Noam. "Overreaching for the Stars of Silicon
Valley." *New York Times*, May 3, 2015, BU6. Retrieved
August 3, 2015 (http://www.nytimes.com/2015/05/03/
upshot/andreessen-horowitz-dealmaker-to-the-stars-of-
silicon-valley.html?abt=0002&abg=0).

Segaller, Stephen. *Nerds 2.0.1: A Brief History of the Internet*.
New York, NY: TV Books, L.L.C., 1999.

SFGate. "On the Record: Marc Andreessen." December 7,
2003. Retrieved June 5, 2015 (http://www.sfgate.com/
business/ontherecord/article/OPSWARE-INC-On-the-
record-Marc-Andreessen-2525822.php).

Sheff, David. "Crank It Up." Wired. August 2000. Retrieved June 5, 2015 (http://archive.wired.com/wired/ archive/8.08/loudcloud.html).

Southwick, Karen. "Andreessen Restarts." Wired, September 2002. Retrieved June 5, 2015 (http://archive.wired.com/ wired/archive/10.09/start.html?pg=17).

Stanford Graduate School of Business. "Laura Arrillaga-An-dreessen: Lecturer in Business Strategy." Retrieved June 5, 2015 (http://www.gsb.stanford.edu/faculty-research/ faculty/laura-arrillaga-andreessen).

Index

About the Author

Corona Brezina is an author who has written more than a dozen young adult books for Rosen Publishing. Several of her previous books have also focused on topics related to science and technology, including *The Scientist's Guide to Physics: Discovering Relativity* and *Internet Biographies: Sergey Brin, Larry Page, Eric Schmidt, and Google*. She lives in Chicago.

Photo Credits

Cover, pp. 1 Chip Somodevilla/Getty Images; pp. 4-5, 85 Michael Kovac/Getty Images; p. 9 MaxyM/Shutterstock.com; p. 11 Kris Connor/Getty Images; p. 12 Stefano Tinti/Shutterstock.com; p. 16 drserg/Shutterstock.com; p. 25 Steve Kagan/Hulton Archive/Getty Images; p. 27 wk1003mike/Shutterstock.com; pp. 29, 56, 64, 66-67, 71, 77, 80-81, 82-83 Bloomberg/Getty Images; p. 32 Robert Burroughs/Hulton Archive/Getty Images; p. 39 Alan Levenson/The LIFE Images Collection/Getty Images; pp. 41, 86-87 © AP Images; p. 43 Mario Tama/Getty Images; p. 47 Rawpixel/Shutterstock.com; p. 49 Brent Stirton/Hulton Archive/Getty Images; p. 53 Justin Sullivan/Getty Images; p. 55 © ZUMA Press, Inc./Alamy; pp. 60-61 Kevork Djansezian/Getty Images; pp. 74-75 Larry Busacca/WireImage/Getty Images; cover and interior pages VikaSuh/Shutterstock.com (light rays), evryka23/iStock/Thinkstock (light grid), Kotkoa/iStock/Thinkstock (circuit) Designer: Brian Garvey; Editor/Photo Researcher: Heather Moore Niver